OUR DAILY BREAD
GUIDE TO EVERYDAY LIFE

OVERCOMING
FEAR
AND
WORRY

JAMES WATKINS

Our Daily Bread
Publishing™

Requests for permission to quote from this book should be directed to: Permissions Department, Our Daily Bread Publishing, PO Box 3566, Grand Rapids, MI 49501, or contact us by email at permissionsdept@odb.org.

Scripture quotations, unless otherwise indicated, are taken from the Holy Bible, New International Version®, NIV®. Copyright © 1973, 1978, 1984, 2011 by Biblica, Inc.™ Used by permission of Zondervan. All rights reserved worldwide. zondervan.com.

Scripture quotations marked NLT are taken from the Holy Bible, New Living Translation, copyright ©1996, 2004, 2015 by Tyndale House Foundation. Used by permission of Tyndale House Publishers, Inc., Carol Stream, Illinois 60188. All rights reserved.

Scripture quotations marked NASB are from the New American Standard Bible®, copyright © 1960, 1962, 1963, 1968, 1971, 1972, 1973, 1975, 1977, 1995 by The Lockman Foundation. Used by permission. (Lockman.org)

Any *italic* in Scripture quotations has been added by the author for emphasis.

Interior design by Michael J. Williams

Library of Congress Cataloging-in-Publication Data

Names: Watkins, James, 1952- author.
Title: Overcoming fear and worry / James N. Watkins.
Description: Grand Rapids : Discovery House, 2019. | Series: Our Daily Bread
    guides to everyday faith | Includes bibliographical references and index.
Identifiers: LCCN 2019000402 | ISBN 9781627079280 (pbk. : alk. paper)
Subjects: LCSH: Worry--Biblical teaching.
Classification: LCC BV4908.5 .W38 2019 | DDC 248.8/6--dc23
LC record available at https://lccn.loc.gov/2019000402

ISBN: 978-1-62707-928-0

Printed in the United States of America
21 22 23 24 25 26 27 28 / 10 9 8 7 6 5 4 3

CONTENTS

YOU ARE NOT ALONE

Hi. I'm Jim. I'm a recovering worrier who has been worry-free for over forty years now. Well, not in a row . . . or even consistently . . . just a total of forty years, here and there, stretched out over sixty years.

I'm assuming you're dealing with your own inconsistent faith and fears or else you'd be reading a book about overcoming Facebook addiction, chocoholism, or pretty much anything other than worry.

My predisposition to worry began at church. Yep, carry-in dinners fed my stomach and my worry habit. Along with Jell-O salads and casserole dishes, the church served up a heaping helping of fear and trembling. For some reason—which I still cannot understand—my childhood church thought it would be great family entertainment to show Civil Defense films. Two memorable titles that kept me awake nights with an upset stomach were *Tips on How to Survive a Nuclear Attack* and a how-to for *The Family Fallout Shelter*.

This was during the Cold War when the United States and the former Soviet Union had thermo-nuclear warheads aimed at each other while they called each other names and had their fingers poised over Launch buttons. Not only did we have fire and tornado drills at school, but we practiced for atomic attack by huddling under our desks. I may have been only six years old, but even I knew a wooden desk was no match for a five-megaton bomb with the power of five million tons of TNT.

Nuclear war and name-calling is still in the news today, along with brand-new fears such as domestic terrorism, school shootings, antibiotic-resistant viruses, the ever-increasing national debt, and . . . well that's probably enough to worry about for now.

And yet Jesus commanded His followers not to worry and not to be afraid.

Like you and me, those in the first century had lots to worry and fret about: high infant mortality rates and a life expectancy of only 35, brutal Roman occupation with oppressive taxes, and government corruption. Many subsisted on two meals a day. Diseases such as bubonic plague, leprosy, typhoid, and tuberculosis, which have since been virtually eliminated, were widespread.

This is the audience to which Jesus commanded, "Do not worry about your life, what you will eat or drink; or about your body, what you will wear" (Matthew 6:25).

So how can you and I live without worry and fear? I'll unpack Jesus's teaching on fear and worry from His Sermon on the Mount. And I'll share practical ways to overcome a problem that has discouraged and oppressed people since Adam confessed, "I was afraid because I was naked." (I still have nightmares about that very same thing.)

Don't worry! You are not alone. And while Jesus's command to not worry or fear is humanly impossible, He provides the superhuman power to obey. So let's begin our journey of overcoming fear and worry.

CHAPTER 1

FEAR FACTOR

Why are you so afraid?

Matthew 8:26

God has designed us with a fight-or-flight response to potentially dangerous situations. Without it, we would never survive outside our crib.

When we are confronted with a six-hundred-pound grizzly bear, for instance, our brain sends out a red alert that instantly releases a flood of hormones including epinephrine (adrenaline) and cortisol, which increases blood pressure and blood sugar as well as stopping digestion and salivation. Arteries dilate to speed this power surge of hormones and blood to the muscles. The blood-clotting function of the body speeds up in order to prevent excessive blood loss. Peripheral vision and hearing decrease so we can laser focus on the massive monster. In a matter of seconds, we are intensely alert, powerful, and able to withstand physical injury.

We are indeed "fearfully and wonderfully made" (Psalm 139:14) to handle short-term threats such as grizzly bears. The key word is *short-term*. That flood of hormones "can be constructive, such as improving performance on a test, sporting event, or public speaking. Although these are normal responses and often helpful responses to danger, anxiety can cause problems when it is turned on too easily, not turned off when danger is absent, or when the response is too strong."[1] If we are continuously reacting to encounters with teddy bears in the same way as the man-eating variety, we become stressed and exhausted. This positive survival mechanism can quickly have a negative effect on our mental and physical states.

The secret is to identify the level of threat. A teddy bear is not a grizzly bear. A minor dustup in a friendship or marriage doesn't spell the end of the relationship. A reprimand from a supervisor doesn't mean you're going to be fired.

I write in my book, *Squeezing Good Out of Bad*, that it's sometimes helpful to identify the intensity of the problem by asking, What would I endure to take this problem away? Is this worry truly a "hand grenade" or is it more in the category of a "hangnail"? You can evaluate it by asking yourself, Would I trade in the elimination of this problem for a hangnail? How 'bout a headache? Harmonica concert? Hernia? Hair loss? Holdup? Hurricane? Hand grenade?[2]

In the grand scheme of life, most worries are somewhere between a harmonica concert and a hernia. But there are moments when I would have eagerly traded some hand-grenade shrapnel for the restoration of a broken relationship or the miraculous resurrection of a loved one. I've had very few hand grenades in my life.

Turning a hangnail into a hand grenade is sometimes referred to as *awfulizing*, a term coined by psychologist Albert Ellis. That stomachache must be stage four cancer. Your friend or spouse being preoccupied can only mean they're intentionally ignoring you. That scraping sound against the siding at midnight is not the wind blowing a branch against the house but the psycho from *Texas Chainsaw Massacre* sawing his way into your home. Our worries get the best of us and take our peace hostage.

We can look at each challenge of life as a hand grenade that threatens to destroy us or as a headache that can prompt us to grow emotionally, spiritually, or mentally. It helps to put life's challenges in perspective.

But just a realistic perspective isn't always enough.

And the Survey Says . . .

A survey by Chapman University randomly samples adults from across the United States to ask their level of fear on a wide variety of topics ranging from crime to natural disasters, the government to the environment, economic concerns to death and illness, aliens to psychic powers.[3] Here are some observations we can make from this study, which is now in its fifth year:

1. *Americans are increasingly fearful.* For the first time in 2018, a majority (over 52 percent) of respondents were fearful of each of the top 12 fears in the list, with the number one fear, corrupt government officials, at 73 percent.
2. *Our fears are not necessarily based on fact.* "Despite evidence to the contrary, Americans do not feel like the United States is becoming a safer place." When asked about crime rates, 2014 participants believed that rates had increased over the last twenty years, although

FBI records show that crime rates had actually decreased.[4]

3. *Our fears are often irrational.* In 2018, more people were afraid of zombies than of either strangers or animals such as dogs and rats.

4. *Our fears are increasingly complex.* On the list we find cyber-terrorism (52 percent) and government use of drones within the US (32 percent), while something so mundane as fear of the dark did not even make the list of 95 possible fears in 2018.

5. *Christians are not exempt from fear.* Of the respondents in the 2018 Chapman fear survey, 54 percent identify themselves as Christian or identify with a Christian denomination, and 32 percent agree the Bible is perfectly true.[5]

The Struggle Is Real

Without a doubt, worry is a significant problem, and has been ever since Eve first worried that God was withholding something good from her.

In Greek—the New Testament's original language—the word *deiliáō* means to be timid or fearful and the word *tarássō* means to agitate, to stir up to cause inward commotion, and to take away calmness of mind. Both are used in John 14:27: "Do not let your hearts be troubled [*tarásso*] and do not be afraid [*deiliáō*]." That sense of agitation is what I still wake up to every morning.

I describe my mind as an EF 5 tornado with thoughts and debris whirling at 300 MPH inside my skull. Everything—news items, events from the previous day, items on my to-do list, people I'm concerned about—all swirl madly in my mind. It's overwhelming, and I have to make a deliberate effort to control it.

You may be experiencing something similar. Your fears may be logical, or not. Your worries may be simple (clowns, anyone?) or complex and layered (illness in the family, financial hardship, broken relationships). You may feel nervous, tense, irritable, and restless—occasionally or regularly—and might have other physical symptoms.*

Maybe you've been a Christian long enough to know that your worrying doesn't accomplish anything. You know in your head that God has the universe within His control. And yet just knowing

---

* **Please note:** Experiencing occasional fear and worry is a normal part of life, and that's what this book is meant to address. If you have frequent, intense, or persistent worry and fear, please talk about that with your primary care physician. This book cannot replace the help of medical professionals and licensed counselors.

doesn't seem to be enough. You seem powerless to help yourself . . .

The good news is, that's exactly where you need to be.

OVERCOMING STEP
Join Worriers Anonymous

The first step in Alcoholics Anonymous is a great way to approach your worries: "I admit that I am powerless over worry—that my life has become unmanageable." Are you having trouble admitting that you're powerless over worry? That's not surprising. Powerlessness is uncomfortable. But when we admit powerlessness before God, we allow His power to go to work. Turn to Him in prayer: "Lord, I am powerless over worry. My life has become unmanageable." Share that with the Lord each time you catch yourself worrying, as many times a day as it takes.

CHAPTER 2

IS WORRY A SIN?

I tell you, do not worry.

Matthew 6:25

As if everyday worries weren't enough, Christians have an additional worry: *Is worry a sin?* I'm glad you asked. There's good news and bad news, but ultimately we'll find encouragement in the answers. Let's get the bad news out of the way first.

The Bad News

Here's what we know:

1. Jesus told His disciples, "If you love me, keep my commands" (John 14:15).

2. Jesus commands "do not worry" two times in Matthew 6.

3. Throughout the Gospels, Jesus tells His followers to "not be afraid," "not fear," "have courage," "take heart," and "be of good cheer" twenty-one times. Two-one! The "Greatest Commandment" to love God and our neighbors only gets *eight* mentions. So, by numbers alone, "fear not" seems to rank as a pretty great commandment as well (and apparently one that needs repeating).

4. Jesus teaches that those who worry are "of little faith" and doing something that "pagans" do (Matthew 6:30, 32). Ouch!

So worrying—if we're completely honest—is disobedience to Jesus and a sign that our love for Him and our faith in Him is not as strong as it should be.

Jesus also notes the danger of worry. In His parable of the sower and the seed, He describes several reactions to the Word of God. Some seed was trampled on the path, some eaten by birds, some fell on rocky soil, and some—thankfully—fell on good soil and yielded a crop one hundred times the amount sown. But Jesus mentions another group of seeds:

Other seed fell among thorns, which grew up
with it and choked the plants. . . .

The seed that fell among thorns stands for
those who hear, but as they go on their way they
are choked by life's worries, riches and plea-
sures, and they do not mature. (Luke 8:7, 14)

So we also see that worry can choke out our spiritual
growth and usefulness in God's work.

Incredibly, Jesus tells us to do things that humans
simply cannot do: do not be angry, do not lust, love
your enemies.[1]

But there's comfort in that too: God's commands
prove to me that the Bible is the holy, inspired Word
of God because no human would ever set these
impossible standards. Doesn't Jesus know what it's
like to be human? Well, yes, He does!

The Good News

Since we have a great high priest who has as-
cended into heaven, Jesus the Son of God, let
us hold firmly to the faith we profess. For we
do not have a high priest who is unable to empathize with our weaknesses, but we have one
who has been tempted in every way, just as we
are—yet he did not sin. Let us then approach

God's throne of grace with confidence, so that we may receive mercy and find grace to help us in our time of need. (Hebrews 4:14–16)

Jesus is the "high priest" who can empathize with our struggles. He understands our human fears and, if we've accepted His sacrifice for our sins, we can confidently find mercy (withholding punishment that we deserve) and grace (blessings that we don't deserve) to help us deal with our sinful worrying. We don't have to do it on our own.

The apostle Peter is Exhibit A for how impossible it is to follow Jesus in our own power. He had enough faith to step out of a boat in the middle of the sea in order to walk on water, and then nearly drowned when he took his eyes off Jesus. He also had a severe case of foot-in-mouth disease, trying to correct Jesus, among other things. And he denied his Savior three times![2] But notice what he writes later in life, after being filled with the Spirit on Pentecost:

His divine power has given us everything we need for a godly life through our knowledge of him who called us by his own glory and goodness. Through these he has given us his very great and precious promises, so that through them you may participate in the divine nature,

having escaped the corruption in the world
caused by evil desires. (2 Peter 1:3–4)

We have what we need to live worry-free through
His power. We can succeed because of *His* glory
and goodness.

But wait! There's more. "Remain in me," Jesus
said, "as I also remain in you" (John 15:4). Jesus
doesn't simply give us the power to live worry-free,
He puts himself in us—Emmanuel, God with Us:

And I will ask the Father, and he will give you
another advocate to help you and *be with you*
forever—the Spirit of truth. The world cannot
accept him, because it neither sees him nor
knows him. But you know him, for *he lives with
you and will be in you.* I will not leave you as
orphans; I will come to you. Before long, the
world will not see me anymore, but you will see
me. Because I live, you also will live. On that day
you will realize that I am in my Father, and you
are in me, and *I am in you.*" (John 14:16–20)

I pray that out of his glorious riches he may
strengthen you with power through his Spirit
in your inner being, so that Christ may *dwell
in your hearts* through faith . . . that you may

be filled to the measure of all the fullness of God.
(Ephesians 3:16–19)

In Jesus's teachings as well as in Paul's writing, it appears the Father, Son, and Spirit fill believers. The Father is in the Son, the Son is in us through the Spirit. No wonder Paul calls this a mystery.[3] What we can know is that we have all of God all the time at our disposal to overcome all worry and fear.

A. B. Simpson, founder of the Christian and Missionary Alliance denomination, writes about this amazing truth:

> The Christian life is not an imitation of Christ, but a direct new creation in Christ, and the union with Christ is so complete that He imparts His own nature to us and lives His own life in us. This, then, is not an imitation but simply the outgrowth of the nature implanted within.
>
> We live Christlike because we have the Christ-life. God is not satisfied with anything less than perfection. He required that from His Son. He requires it from us, and He does not, in the process of grace, reduce the standard, but He brings us up to it.[4]

While other religions seek after a higher power somewhere out there, God the Father, Son, and

Spirit seeks us out and chooses to live within us. That is harder for me to comprehend than the whole 100% God–100% human, three-in-one, infinite in time and space things. And yet that is exactly what His Word teaches.

Someone has tried to explain this mystery as a bottle without a cap submerged in the ocean. The ocean is in the bottle and the bottle is in the ocean. God is infinite—beyond the farthest reaches of the universe—and yet is inside these finite bodies.

As followers of Jesus Christ, we have all of God within our beings, but the question is, does God have all of us? As we grow in our faith, we allow more and more of God's Spirit to direct our thoughts, actions, and words. Again, a more mature Peter writes:

> His divine power has given us everything we need for a godly life through our knowledge of him who called us by his own glory and goodness. Through these he has given us his very great and precious promises, so that through them you may participate in the divine nature, having escaped the corruption in the world caused by evil desires.
>
> For this very reason, make every effort to add to your faith goodness; and to goodness, knowledge; and to knowledge, self-control;

and to self-control, perseverance; and to per-severance, godliness; and to godliness, mutual affection; and to mutual affection, love. For if you possess these qualities in increasing mea-sure, they will keep you from being ineffective and unproductive in your knowledge of our Lord Jesus Christ. But whoever does not have them is nearsighted and blind, forgetting that they have been cleansed from their past sins. (2 Peter 1:3–9)

So these qualities don't derive from us, but from a holy God living within us. For instance, God doesn't give us love, He gives us himself:

Dear friends, let us love one another, for love comes from God. Everyone who loves has been born of God and knows God. Whoever does not love does not know God, because God is love. . . .

No one has ever seen God; but if we love one another, *God lives in us* and his love is made complete in us. (1 John 4:7–8, 12)

In the same way, God the Son does not give us peace from worry—He is peace: "Now may the Lord of peace himself give you peace at all times and in every way. The Lord be with all of you" (2 Thessalonians 3:16).

He puts himself in us so we can do the humanly impossible! Many of the principles in this book for dealing with worry will work for everyone, everywhere. But only those who have accepted the Son of God as their Lord and Savior have the God of love, peace, and power living within them. So they are uniquely equipped to obey the command, Do not worry.

Think about Christ's strange answer to the disciples' request, "Show us how to increase our faith":

> If you had faith even as small as a mustard seed, you could say to this mulberry tree, "May you be uprooted and be planted in the sea," and it would obey you! (Luke 17:5–6 NLT)

Jesus ignores the specific request and implies the amount isn't the issue. The issue is whether we have faith or not. It's binary—an either/or—in the same way a woman is either pregnant or not pregnant.

We see this when a father brings his son, writhing and foaming at the mouth, to Jesus and pleads:

> "If you can do anything, take pity on us and help us."

"'If you can'?" said Jesus. "Everything is possible for one who believes."

Immediately the boy's father exclaimed, "I do believe; help me overcome my unbelief!" (Mark 9:22–24)

And the Verdict Is . . .

So to answer the question, "Is worry a sin?" I would have to answer yes. The Greek word translated "falling short" in Romans 3:23 is *hamartia*. It helps us understand what sin is: falling short of God's glorious standard. Paul uses the same Greek word in his stern warning, "For the wages of sin [*hamartia*] is death, but the gift of God is eternal life in Christ Jesus our Lord" (Romans 6:23).

Clearly, this sin can't be taken lightly. It is a deadly sin that Jesus died for, and we need His forgiveness on a daily basis.

So I invite you to join my virtual support group and confess, "Hi, I'm _____. I'm a worrier." Hear the confessions of these fear-filled worriers who are part of our circle:

David: "My adversaries pursue me all day long; . . . When I am afraid, I put my trust in God."

Daniel: "I, Daniel, was the only one who saw the vision; those who were with me did not see it, but such terror overwhelmed them that they fled and hid themselves. So I was left alone, gazing at this great vision; I had no strength left, my face turned deathly pale and I was helpless."

The disciples: "Jesus said to us, 'You of little faith, why are you so afraid?'"

Peter: "But when I saw the wind, I was afraid and, beginning to sink, cried out, 'Lord, save me!'"

Women disciples: "On Easter morning, we hurried away from the tomb, afraid yet filled with joy, and ran to tell his disciples."

Paul: "One night the Lord spoke to me in a vision: 'Do not be afraid; keep on speaking, do not be silent.' . . . I am afraid that when I go to visit churches I may not find them as I want them to be, and they may not find me as they want me to be. I fear that there may be discord, jealousy, fits of rage, selfish ambition, slander, gossip, arrogance, and disorder."[5]

You and I are not alone. Even devout believers in Christ are not exempt from fear. Yes, worry is a sin, but it is not unpardonable. If we're being honest, we have to admit we fall short of God's glory on a consistent and regular basis: "If we claim to be without sin [*hamartia*], we deceive ourselves and the truth is not in us. If we confess our sins, he is faithful and just and will forgive us our sins and purify us from all unrighteousness" (1 John 1:8–9).

The good news is that God can not only "forgive" our worrying, but "purify us" from it as we'll learn in the remaining chapters.

OVERCOMING STEP
Admit your sin

Admit that worry is a sin that disobeys specific commands of Jesus Christ and ask Him for forgiveness. When you're tempted to worry today, personalize 2 Thessalonians 3:16—*May the Lord of peace give me peace at all times and in every way*—and be open to the Spirit's power within you to overcome your fears.

CHAPTER 3

BUT . . .

And why do you worry?

Matthew 6:28

Most of us are able to admit that our worry and fear is sinful, but that admission alone isn't enough to stop us. In Jesus's Sermon on the Mount, He asks, "Why do you worry?" Most of us are armed with one or more responses to that. *I know I shouldn't worry, but . . .*

It's Just Who I Am!

You might be one of those people who seem to just be a natural-born worrier. Like me, you may have plenty of stories about childhood fears and worries. Every Saturday morning as a child, I would buckle my gun belt, adjust my black mask, and drag my rocking horse in front of the black-and-white TV. At precisely 11 a.m., I would hear, "A hearty 'Hi Ho, Silver,' the Lone Ranger rides again!" I watched enthralled as "the masked rider of the plains led the fight for law and order in the early west."

And every Saturday morning, I ended up hiding under the coffee table worried as *kemosabe* and his faithful companion, Tonto, were tied up in an abandoned mine. Dynamite's fuse burning down. Surrounded by twenty armed desperadoes. My first-grade mind couldn't conceive of any possible escape.

My mother would shove the *TV Guide* under the table. "See, the *Lone Ranger* is scheduled for next Saturday. He's got to get of the mine alive." But the facts didn't make much difference to my worry.

It is true that the "nature" aspect can certainly play a part in your worry problem today. Studies suggest, for instance, that if a mother was under a lot of stress during her pregnancy, her elevated stress hormones could affect her unborn child, causing a variety of problems, including an increased risk of anxiety into adulthood.[1] Or it could be a matter of "nurture," where the home you were raised in was somehow unstable. If you grew up in an atmosphere of stress—whether influenced by abuse, abandonment, poverty, neglect, mental health issues, or parental discord—your inclination toward worry and fear is increased. Or if you grew up in a home that demanded perfection in everything—school work, sports, good citizenship—you may also live with the worry that you're not measuring up to your family's impossible standards, and you may have adopted that mind-set yourself and are now worried that your home and family aren't living up to your own perfectionist tendencies. Worry can be a vicious cycle.

I'm Not Feeling Well!

Have you ever had the experience where your body feels worried or fearful, even though your head can't figure out why? There are lots of potential triggers for those physical responses. Believe it or not, it could be as simple as skipping breakfast. Your body interprets this hunger as the precursor to starvation, so your body raises your level of cortisol and kicks the stress response in motion. And if you satisfy your hunger with a sugary snack or drink, your insulin level spikes with the increase of blood sugar, further stressing out your body. Eating breakfast with good-quality protein and fat—and avoiding sugar—actually lowers nervous stress.

Food allergies and environmental toxins can also compound feelings of fear. For instance, if you are gluten intolerant and eat something with gluten, your body treats the inflammation as a crisis and initiates the stress response.

Viral infections can also stimulate the stress response, and vice versa, as a constant state of worry can weaken your immune system. Lack of sleep, digestive problems, headaches . . . all these can both cause worry and be the symptoms of worry. Have I mentioned worry can be a vicious cycle?

There are multiple other physical causes for the onset of anxiety disorders, which this book is not meant to address. Family history, certain diseases and other disorders, medications—the list goes on. If you suspect that what you're experiencing is more than just garden-variety fear or worry, it's important to get help early from a medical professional. (See the appendix for a fuller discussion of the difference between *worry* and *anxiety*.)

I Just Want to Be Prepared!

Seth J. Gillihan, professor of psychology in the psychiatry department at the University of Pennsylvania, believes "Each time we worry and nothing bad happens, our mind connects worry with preventing harm." So we subconsciously conclude, "It's a good thing I worried."[2]

We may worry through all the possible outcomes of a given situation, even bracing ourselves to expect the worst, so that we're not surprised. This type of worry may be concealing a bigger fear—a fear of the unknown or a fear of not being in control of a situation. Dr. Gillihan explains: "Our beliefs about worry can have a superstitious element because we believe that the act of worrying itself somehow lowers the likelihood of a dreaded outcome. We might think that if we stop worrying we'd be inviting trouble."[3] Somehow worrying makes us feel like we're in control.

I saw that very thing when we flew with our two-year-old daughter, Faith. I could tell the passenger sitting to my right was a first-time flier. He actually read the safety card—twice. He listened attentively as the flight attendant explained the operation of the seat belt. As the pilot revved the engines and released the brakes, taking us from zero to two hundred miles per hour, Faith buried her head into my chest. However, the man next to me was actually pulling his armrests up as he was helping lift the nearly five-hundred-ton 747 off the runway. Two different reactions—neither of which had any effect on the takeoff.

I Only Worry Because I Care!

Some world-class worriers can be very pious about their worrying: "I only worry because I *care*." Dr. Gillihan notes that there's a huge difference "between caring about a situation—including doing everything in our power to help it turn out well—and worrying needlessly and fruitlessly about it."[4] So, a show of hands. How many of you have scolded a loved one for getting home late? "Do you know how much I worried about you? You could have been dead on the side of the road!" I don't think I'm the only one raising my hand.

I'm Under Stress!

The more of life's stresses that pile on, the more there is to worry about, right? And it's natural to worry when we're under stress, right?

Sometimes worry feels productive. It can help us get things done. That adrenaline surge helps us stay up later and work faster. I have writer friends who don't feel motivated to write until the deadline is looming and the editor is breathing down their neck. A little fear gets them in gear. At least for me, worry stifles my creativity.

Some people believe that worry not only motivates them but inspires them to solve problems.

Dr. Gillihan writes, "We might tell ourselves that worrying is how we find solutions to our problems. However, extreme worry is more likely to *interfere* with problem-solving. Once more, we need to be aware of the difference between productive problem-solving and wheel-spinning worry."[5] Bottom line: worry is unproductive.

Have you ever thought or said one or more of these reasons for worry? We may have very good physical, psychological, emotional, or circumstantial reasons for our worry, but that doesn't make living in fear okay. God doesn't say, "I tell you, do not worry unless you have good reason." Is it a good excuse to say, It's just how I've always been? No. No more than if you'd always been angry or violent. We're all born in sin, and it's not an excuse.

But worrying out of concern for someone else is okay, right? Imagine if this passage were in Scripture: "Praise be to the God and Father of our Lord Jesus Christ, the Father of fear and the God of all worry, who worries with us in all our troubles, so that we can worry with those in any trouble with the fear we ourselves receive from God" (horrifically adapted from 2 Corinthians 1:3–4). No, no, and no. What's helpful is compassion and comfort—the words these verses really use.

In our virtual support group today, let's commit to setting aside excuses. Who wants to start? How about you, David?

David: "Why, my soul, are you downcast? Why so disturbed within me? Put your hope in God, for I will yet praise him, my Savior and my God."[6]

OVERCOMING STEP
Stop making excuses

How do you rationalize your worry? Make a list—just this once—of the reasons you worry. Then, pray over your list, asking God to help you set aside your excuses.

CHAPTER 4

WORRIED SICK

Can any one of you by worrying add a single hour to your life?

Matthew 6:27

Jesus warns us that worrying can't add a single hour to our lives. But worse, it can *subtract* hours—and years.

As we talked about in chapter 1, our bodies are designed for prompt fight-or-flight reactions, but not for prolonged stretches of red alert. In our fast-paced, giving 110 percent, workaholic environment, we can feel stuck in fight-or-flight. The grizzly bears of a packed calendar, high-pressure sales meetings, competitive social lives, and tense relationships with friends and family members don't allow for our bodies to return to the necessary resting state. (I actually took a month off from writing after finishing this book. I needed a break!)

God has designed us for a rhythm of work and rest. He gave us night for sleep. He gave us the Sabbath for rest so that every week we would get one whole day to rest from our work. (Think about it: If you don't take off one day a week, you're breaking one of God's top ten commandments.) Our minds and bodies are simply not made for the modern-day, 24/7 pace of life.

I had a very creative friend who decided that his electric train needed more power than the transformer was delivering. So he cut off the end of an extension cord, wrapped the two exposed wires to the tracks, and plugged it in. (Do I really need to say, "Do not try this at home"?) His model train engine shot down the straightaway at warp speed before bursting into flames. The electric motor was designed for twelve volts, not one hundred twenty.

Unfortunately, we do the same thing. We power our bodies with enough espresso, energy drinks, and mental stimulation to power a T. Rex in a triathlon—and then wonder why we feel burned out.

If we listen, our bodies will warn us when we're resisting God's design and disobeying His Word.

Truth or Consequences

A lifestyle of high-speed worry has serious consequences on the body's systems: cardiovascular, respiratory, digestive, immune, and others. The fight-or-flight response is perfect for immediate physical fears—a mugger, a rabid dog, a house fire—but not for mental fears—a huge medical bill, kids driving home in a snowstorm, or having blood drawn. Those fight-or-flight hormones build up, but the body has nowhere to run and nothing to fight, so they can harm the body. An increased heart rate and gorged blood vessels are just fine for running from the grizzly bear, for instance, but prolonged they can lead to high blood pressure and cardiovascular disease. Anxiety literally "weighs down the heart" (Proverbs 12:25). Ongoing fear and worry can contribute to a wide range of problems:

- diarrhea and other digestive issues
- dizziness
- fatigue
- frequent illness
- headaches
- high blood pressure
- inability to concentrate

- insomnia
- irritability
- loss of appetite
- loss of libido
- muscle aches and tension
- rapid breathing and shortness of breath
- rapid heart rate, palpitations, or chest pain
- stomachaches, nausea
- trembling, tics, twitching

And if left unaddressed, uncontrolled worry can lead to depression, anxiety disorders, and even cause heart attacks.

The first step to staying healthy is awareness. For example, knowing that those "butterflies" we feel in our stomachs before a test, a meeting with the boss, or a public talk are actually your digestive system shutting down due to worry can help you understand that sensation at other times. Knowing that if we find ourselves in a long-term state of fight-or-flight, our bodies don't get the all-clear signal and they remain on high alert, weakening our immune system, we can take extra precautions against illness. The key is paying attention to our body's cues.

While waiting in pre-op for a cancer biopsy, the nurse asked, as she took my blood pressure, "Are you nervous?"

"Uh, I don't think so."

She looked at the numbers, scowled, and announced, "actually, you *are* nervous. Your body doesn't lie."

Worry can lead to physical symptoms and physical symptoms can make us worry, and next thing we know, we're on the worry-go-round and are desperate to jump off. Fortunately, there is much we can do to diminish or completely eliminate the physical *causes* of stress as well as help alleviate the physical *effects* of worry.

Really Rest

We need rest. As we sleep, our body and mind are actually repairing themselves. Our brain is working to sort and organize what we learned during the day. To use a computer term, our brain is *defragging*: deleting duplicate files, organizing similar material into the same files, and making sure it is running quickly and efficiently. And, to use another computer concept, your brain is working on problems in the background as you sleep. Hence the old advice to "sleep on it"; we often wake up with a solution.

Sleep also boosts our creativity, as our rested brain can more easily tap into our unconscious thoughts.

Meanwhile, your body is releasing hormones that stimulate tissue growth. This also helps the body recover from injuries such as cuts, scrapes, and stressed muscles. During sleep, your body is also busy producing more white blood cells that attack infections and viruses. This is why doctors often prescribe bed rest.

But wait, there's more!

Dr. Eric Olson of the Mayo Clinic writes, "Lack of sleep can affect your immune system. Studies show that people who don't get quality sleep or enough sleep are more likely to get sick after being exposed to a virus, such as a common cold virus. Lack of sleep can also affect how fast you recover if you do get sick."[1] Your body naturally lowers your stress hormones during sleep, which may inhibit inflammations that are linked to heart disease and lower blood sugar, among other things.

Your heart also gets a bit of a break during sleep as your blood pressure drops.

And sleep is a mood enhancer. "When you don't get the seven to nine hours of quality sleep you need, it can heavily influence your outlook on life, energy level, motivation, and emotions. If you're feeling low, you may not realize that lack of sleep is the culprit."[2]

To make the most of all these great benefits of sleep, here are some practical tips to shift from fight-or-flight mode into that relaxed and regenerate state.

Turn off all electronic devices—phone, TV, computer—one hour before bed. If you get a critical email or text right before bed, you're going to be tossing all night devising the perfect solution or put-them-in-their-place response. If you fall asleep to the news, your mind will be filled with the latest murder, political uprising, or stock market drop. If you use your phone for an alarm clock, at least turn it facedown to avoid the light which tells your pineal gland it's time to get up.

Consider keeping all electronic devices out of the bedroom, period. If your bedroom is only used for sleep and "sleeping with" your spouse, your body will associate the bedroom only with rest and pleasure. It can't be a relaxing, refreshing refuge if murder, mayhem, or office work also occupy the space.

Cultivate Composure

Here's a simple formula for reducing stress, worry, and global climate change. (Okay, maybe not melting ice caps.)

$$Y Z > A R = C$$

Simply put, if the amount of your zeal (YZ) is greater than your area of responsibility (AR), then you will experience composure (C).

For instance, Kevin has the zeal and energy of the Energizer Bunny on speed, so let's say he has 10 "Z-factors" for his amount of energy and zeal (YZ). He's married, the father of two, works 60-plus hours per week as a nuclear power operator, and serves as a member of the county school board for a score of 9 for areas of responsibility (AR). As long as his amount of zeal (10) is greater than his areas of responsibility (9), he will experience "composure."

Let's say that Elizabeth is a working mom (is there any other kind?) with two preschoolers; she volunteers at the local crisis pregnancy center and is guardian of her aging parents, so she also has a 9 for areas of responsibility. But—*uh-oh*—her Z-factor is only a 7. Because her amount of zeal (YZ) is less than her area of responsibility (AR), the $Y Z > A R = C$ equation is reversed and, instead of composure (C), she feels like she's going . . .

$$C = R A > Z Y$$

The Z-Factor Theory, then, is quite simple. If we're going to maintain composure in our lives—and avoid being ordered to see a court-appointed psychiatrist—our energy level needs to be greater than our areas of responsibility. By recognizing that each person's metabolism and personality equip them with a unique amount of zeal, we can make an effort not to go over our own area of responsibility weight limit. On a practical level, there are two ways to assure this: increase our level of zeal or decrease our areas of responsibility.

It is possible to maximize our natural energy and enthusiasm by getting adequate sleep, eating right, and exercising every morning.

Once our zeal is maximized, it needs to be harnessed and directed. A personal mission statement can help us identify where our zeal will be focused, clarifying what we are willing to accept as our areas of responsibility. My mission statement is, "to communicate the gospel of Christ in an effective and creative manner and with as many people as possible" based on Matthew 28:19–20.

Avoid Overload

Once we know our limits and have a focused idea of what our God-given areas of responsibility should be, we can easily apply the D-4 Formula to keep from overloading our lives.

D1. *Don't.* Try this very simple exercise. Standing upright in a relaxed position, take a deep breath, and as you exhale say, "No." You may need to practice this in front of a mirror or with a friend, but it is easier than drinking raw eggs with bee pollen and running ten miles every day.

By having a mission statement that we sense God has given us, we can more easily say, "Thanks so much for asking, but I'll have to say no." And most important, we're not doing things God never intended us to do.

For instance, as soon as my church district learned I was a writer, I was asked to be the secretary of their board of administration. The monthly meetings were an hour drive away and usually lasted three hours. By simply saying no, I freed up sixty hours a year to spend doing what I do well: writing.

There's nothing in Scripture that requires you to say yes to every volunteer plea at your workplace, school, or church. (I can write you a note for your pastor if you wish.) If it doesn't fit your mission statement and talents, you shouldn't be doing it.

To quote drug prevention programs, "Just say no." This wonderful time-saving device keeps our ARs manageable, and minimizes worry!

D2. *Delegate.* If someone else has more time and more talent for a particular project, defer or delegate the task—even if you feel you could do it better! First Corinthians 12 teaches that every part of the body of Christ—even the "weaker" and "less honorable" and "unpresentable"—have important and indispensable roles in the work of the church.

Likewise, at work, you are only accountable for your own job, no one else's. And contrary to what your teen may be telling you, child labor laws do not apply to your own flesh and blood. My brother and I never, ever said, "We're bored," because we would immediately find a snow shovel, garden hoe, or rake in our hands. Chores are a wonderful way for your children to learn a work ethic and for you to reduce your AR and worries.

D3. *Delay.* There are some real advantages to delaying a task or project a while.

1. By delaying, we may not have to do it at all. I never start to seriously work on a speech for a conference until about a week before the meeting. Recently two conferences have been cancelled because of budget problems. Fortunately I hadn't spent months preparing a talk for a seminar that never materialized.

2. By delaying, our subconscious has time to work on the task. When I'm working on an article or speaking assignment, I tell that little creative muse inside my head, "Don't bother me with your ideas right now. Keep working on it, and I'll get back with you closer to the deadline." It's amazing—and sometimes frightening—the work our subconscious creativity can produce when given enough time. Ideas just pour out of my little head!

3. By delaying, we avoid wasting time. The principle that "work expands to fill the time allotted" is so true. A meeting scheduled for three hours will take three hours to deal with the agenda items; if it's scheduled for an hour and a half, it will take an hour and a half to deal with the same agenda.

Delaying a task, however, is *not* the same as procrastinating or just putting it off. Rather, we allow adequate time to do the task well, but don't give it more time than it deserves.

4. And, of course, the best reason of all. Jesus could return before that deadline!

D4. *Do.* If we can't say no, can't delegate, and can't delay, then we must *do.* But if we've kept our ARs below our Z-factors, we'll have enough energy to complete our responsibilities with a degree of composure and fewer worries.

So, when you feel your "composure" degenerating into "crazy," ask God to give you wisdom in applying these principles. Jesus never said, "Blessed are the frazzled, for they shall earn points with God." Rather, He promises, "My yoke is easy to bear, and the burden I give you is light" (Matthew 11:30 NLT). Don't take on more responsibility than you sense God is giving you.

God has already provided the work-rest rhythm; now we need to choose to live by His design. We need to trust that He knows what's best for us.

OVERCOMING STEP
Rest in God's design

Meditate on Matthew 11:28–30. Ask God if there's a specific mission statement for your life that will help you focus your areas of responsibility and allow your body the rest it needs. Make at least one needed change this week.

CHAPTER 5

TO WORRY
OR NOT TO WORRY

*Look at the birds of the air. . . . Are you not much
more valuable than they?*

Matthew 6:26

I hate God's guts." Nick had recently started attend-
ing the youth group and had wanted to talk after
Bible study. One thing I quickly learned as a young
youth pastor was that teens always ask a test question. And then, if you don't totally freak out with the
first question, they will ask you their real question.

"So, tell me what you hate about God."

"You've been talking about how God is our heavenly father. Well, if He's my heavenly father, I hate
his guts."

"So, tell me about your earthly father."

"My old man's a drunken [expletive]. He beats my mom and when he gets bored with that, he beats me. One time, he stripped me down, threw me out the back door into the snow, and turned the hose on me. I hate his guts."

It was not hard to understand how Nick could not wrap his head around the truth that God was a father who loved him.

"So, who's your favorite TV father?"

"What?"

"Who's your favorite TV father?"

"Uh, I guess Andy Taylor—the sheriff from Mayberry."

"Yeah, he's a great father. So now, I want you to imagine that God is Andy Taylor times infinity. He loves you infinitely more than you can imagine. In fact, He wants us to enjoy a relationship with Him and others that is 'good, pleasing, and perfect' (Romans 12:2)."

Nick cocked his head and looked serious. Then he said, "Cool!" and bounded off to join his friends.

You Are Loved

Perhaps you're struggling with worry because you're not quite sure that God really does love you and wants what is good, pleasing, and perfect for you. Maybe an earthly father has let you down, deserted you, or even abused you.

Whatever the image our earthly father has created, Scripture demonstrates that God loves us more than even the most perfect TV father:

The LORD your God is with you,
   the Mighty Warrior who saves.
He will take great delight in you;
   in his love he will no longer rebuke you,
   but will rejoice over you with singing.
                     (Zephaniah 3:17)

For God so loved the world that he gave his one and only Son, that whoever believes in him shall not perish but have eternal life.
                     (John 3:16)

You see, at just the right time, when we were still powerless, Christ died for the ungodly. Very rarely will anyone die for a righteous person, though for a good person someone might possibly dare to die. But God demonstrates his own love for us in this: While we were still sinners, Christ died for us.
                 (Romans 5:6–8)

My command is this: Love each other as I have loved you. Greater love has no one than this: to lay down one's life for one's friends. You are my friends if you do what I command. I no longer call you servants, because a servant does not know his master's business. Instead, I have called you friends.

(John 15:12–15)

For I am convinced that neither death nor life, neither angels nor demons, neither the present nor the future, nor any powers, neither height nor depth, nor anything else in all creation, will be able to separate us from the love of God that is in Christ Jesus our Lord.

(Romans 8:38–39)

Wow! We are loved. Do you believe that? If you're worried, it may be that you're not sure you really are loved. You're afraid that God is going to let you down.

If you're a dad, you've probably hoisted your toddler on top of the dresser (or wall or edge of the swimming pool), stepped back and urged, "Jump to Daddy. Daddy will catch you." Although Mommy may not approve, it's a powerful lesson of being able to trust someone who loves you.

I remember the discussion with my oldest grandson when he was perched on the monkey bars and was afraid to come down.

"Jump, and I'll catch you."

"No!"

"Why not?"

"You won't catch me."

"Have I ever *not* caught you before?"

"No. But what if you miss and drop me?"

"Have I *ever* dropped you before?"

"No but . . ."

The conversation went on another five minutes as we discussed my credibility and ability to catch him. Eventually, he closed his eyes and jumped into my arms—and I dropped him on his head. No, of course not! I caught him and hugged him tight.

My oldest granddaughter, who is just eight days younger, was always jumping off things and trusting me to catch her. We had been her regular babysitters since she was born, so she was used to seeing us for entire days a few times a week. She had learned from birth that "Papaw" loved her, was dependable, and would do everything in his power to keep her from getting hurt. But because our grandson lives a distance away, we only got to see him once a month.

The better we know someone, the more we can predict how they will respond. Like Nick, who believed his father didn't have his best interests at heart. Our granddaughter knew I loved her. And so, if kids know Daddy as a strong protector, they will take that jump from atop the dresser, and land in Daddy's strong, loving embrace. Then they'll squeal, "Do it again!" until Daddy—or Papaw—is completely exhausted.

I love the J. B. Phillips paraphrase of 1 Peter 5:7: "You can throw the whole weight of your anxieties upon him, for you are his personal concern."[1]

King David writes, "Cast your cares on the LORD and he will sustain you; he will never let the righteous be shaken" (Psalm 55:22). The Hebrew word *shâlak* translated "cast" here, literally means to throw, cast off, or toss out. Jump off the dresser, throw the whole weight of your anxieties on Him— because God loves you unconditionally.

I do most of my serious worrying in the middle of the night. I'll be sleeping soundly when I suddenly wake up with the crisis of the week whirling in my mind. At 3:00 a.m., I probably can't—or at least shouldn't—send a text or email or make a phone call. Businesses and organizations are closed. And, unless there's a fire, my wife is not going to be happy to be awakened. So I'm left holding this huge burden on my own. I've gone to envisioning the problem wrapped up as a huge package. I whisper,

"God, you ask us to cast our cares on you, so . . ." And then I actually mime picking up the package and hurling it out of bed.

My daughter, a licensed therapist, asks her clients to do the same thing. In the middle of the group, there is an imaginary bucket. As they describe past failures or shortcomings, they are encouraged to "chuck it in the bucket." That is exactly what the psalmist is instructing us to do: chuck it in the bucket.

Jesus clearly teaches that His Father—and ours— is not going to drop us when we chuck ourselves into His arms:

> Which of you fathers, if your son asks for a fish, will give him a snake instead? Or if he asks for an egg, will give a scorpion? If you then, though you are evil, know how to give good gifts to your children, how much more will your Father in heaven give the Holy Spirit to those who ask him! (Luke 11:11–13)

I do need to make a disclaimer here. Sometimes it seems the Father does drop us on our heads. Sometimes it seems we get a scorpion. You know what I'm talking about. I devoted a third of a recent book to discussing unanswered prayer. To give you the much-abridged version of it, "God is all-wise. We're not." God seems to answer prayer—and He *always* answers—in one of three ways represented by a traffic signal. Green is go. The thing we're asking is good for us. Yellow is slow. The thing may be good for us—but not now. And red is no. It won't be good for us—ever.

It's a bit more complicated than that, but for now, let's agree that if we ask for a snake, God in His love and wisdom isn't going to give it to us if what we really need is a fish.

It's the same kind of love that you exhibit when you take your little ones for their childhood vaccinations. Your kids are going to think you are the meanest parent in the whole wide world to allow them to be tortured with needles. What they can't understand is that diphtheria, mumps, and polio are far worse—and potentially deadlier—than a needle prick.

You Are Loved—And Valued

While I was serving as campus pastor at a Christian university, Darla dropped by my office, slumped in the chair in front of my desk, and sighed, "I'm worthless."

"Really? Tell me why."

She told—in graphic detail—about a lifetime of being raped by both her father and her brother.

"I'm worthless. No one is going to want me as a dirty, used piece of meat."

I tried to maintain my poker-faced, objective counselor persona, but all I could say is, "I am so sorry, Darla. So very sorry."

For the rest of the semester Darla and I looked at Scriptures that assured her that she was valuable—even before birth:

> So God created human beings in his own
> image.
>   In the image of God he created them;
>   male and female he created them.
>   (Genesis 1:27 NLT)

> For you created my inmost being;
>   you knit me together in my mother's womb.
> I praise you because I am fearfully and won-
>   derfully made;
>   your works are wonderful,
>   I know that full well.
> My frame was not hidden from you
>   when I was made in the secret place . . .
>   (Psalm 139:13–15)

In Jesus's teaching about not worrying, He affirms our value:

Are not five sparrows sold for two pennies? Yet not one of them is forgotten by God. Indeed, the very hairs of your head are all numbered. Don't be afraid; you are worth more than many sparrows. (Luke 12:6–7)

Birds do not worry because God provides for them. He has built into their DNA the knowledge to fly south in the winter and how to return to the same backyard every spring for a ready supply of food. All that care in creating a two-cent sparrow.

Jesus then goes on to note that God has the very hairs of our heads numbered; we are much more valuable than our feathered friends.

The Living Bible paraphrases Psalm 139:17–18, "How precious it is, Lord, to realize that you are thinking about me constantly! I can't even count how many times a day your thoughts turn toward me. And when I waken in the morning, you are still thinking of me!"[2]

I've always wondered how God can be thinking of over seven billion people at the very same time. Being eternal and not being bound by time may be part of the secret. But then I read about a Chinese supercomputer that can perform thirty-four quadrillion calculations per second. A quadrillion is one thousand trillion. So, if chips of silicon can do that, then God can easily be thinking about over seven billion individual people every second of every day.

But our ultimate value is in the price Christ paid to redeem us!

> For you know that it was not with perishable things such as silver or gold that you were redeemed from the empty way of life handed down to you from your ancestors, but with the precious blood of Christ, a lamb without blemish or defect. (1 Peter 1:18–19)

You Are Loved, Valued . . . And Disciplined

Although we are infinitely loved and valued, the loving Father is not going to approve of us doing anything that will be less than loving toward Him and others. Jesus supplied these as the two greatest commandments:

> "The most important one," answered Jesus, "is this: 'Hear, O Israel: The Lord our God, the Lord is one. Love the Lord your God with all your heart and with all your soul and with all your mind and with all your strength.' The

second is this: 'Love your neighbor as yourself.'
There is no commandment greater than these."
(Mark 12:29–31)

And the apostle Paul reiterated:

"Love your neighbor as yourself." Love does
no harm to a neighbor. Therefore love is the
fulfillment of the law. (Romans 13:9–10)

To violate these commandments is sin. Because
of the Father's love, He treats us like any good parent in disciplining us:

And have you forgotten the encouraging words
God spoke to you as his children? He said,

"My child, don't make light of the LORD's
discipline,
    and don't give up when he corrects you.
For the LORD disciplines those he loves,
    and he punishes each one he accepts as his
child." . . .
For our earthly fathers disciplined us for a
few years, doing the best they knew how. But
God's discipline is always good for us, so that
we might share in his holiness. No discipline

is enjoyable while it is happening—it's painful! But afterward there will be a peaceful harvest of right living for those who are trained in this way. (Hebrews 12:5–6, 10–11 NLT)

I think one way our heavenly Father disciplines us is with His timing. We have human deadlines when we need the money for the utilities, car repairs, or the Internal Revenue Service. Other times there's a task we need to accomplish by a certain date set by our school, employer, or even church. But I've found that my human deadlines don't seem to matter in divine timing. I may need the mortgage paid by the first of the month, but a week later—after fervent prayer and fasting—I still don't have the money for the payment.

Here's what I think God is doing (although He's never invited me to a planning meeting). I believe that it is in that period between the human deadline and God's deliverance that our faith grows.

If God were a vending machine in which I placed my prayer and the answer came out every time—immediately—I would soon take Him for granted. I might pound on the machine if it didn't vend my needs promptly. God promises to meet our needs. He doesn't promise overnight delivery. Or as my friend Aron Willis likes to say, "God will never let you down—but He'll scare you to death."

You Are Loved, Valued, and Disciplined, So You Don't Need to Worry

Looking back on my childhood, I don't recall ever being scared or worried about food, drink, clothing, or shelter. My dad, at times, worked two jobs to provide for a stay-at-home mom and two boys who were forever outgrowing their jeans and sneakers. My mom was the original Martha Stewart, making wonderful meals from the vegetables we grew in our one-acre garden, sewing creative Halloween costumes, and scrubbing the kitchen clean enough to be commandeered for a M.A.S.H. surgical unit.

I didn't realize that never having store-bought canned fruits and vegetables, frozen dinners, and cakes from mixes was a sign of tough financial times. We simply rejoiced in home-cooked meals and amazing desserts from scratch. We call this "blissful ignorance." When we don't know what's wrong, or what could potentially go wrong, it's pretty easy to be worry-free.

Jesus gives us the opportunity to reclaim this kind of comforting dependency. We can release our worries as we rely on God's provision. With a little child as an object lesson, He told his disciples:

> Truly I tell you, unless you change and become like little children, you will never enter

the kingdom of heaven. Therefore, whoever takes the lowly position of this child is the greatest in the kingdom of heaven. (Matthew 18:3–4)

The disciples' (and our) security and success in the kingdom was not going to be based on what they accomplished but would be based on their dependence on Christ to accomplish everything.

Worry is a glaring warning sign that we are resisting childlike dependence on Him. I can feel I'm a patient person . . . until someone cuts me off in traffic. I can believe I'm a humble person . . . until someone takes the credit I deserve. And in the same way, I can feel I have faith . . . until, well, any number of worry triggers.

Worry can mean . . .

- I question God's love for me.
- I doubt my value to Him.
- I disbelieve His power.
- I wonder if He really has my best interest in mind.

Remember, Christ's presence gives us the power to live out His commands:

For you were buried with Christ when you were baptized. And with him you were raised to new life because you trusted the mighty power of God, who raised Christ from the dead (Colossians 2:12 NLT).

We have the power to resist worry, if we're willing to accept it. We are loved, valued, and disciplined by a heavenly Father, so we don't have to be worried.

OVERCOMING STEP
Throw yourself into the Father's loving arms

Make a list of all the ways God has shown His love to you, has shown that He values you, and, as a caring Father, has disciplined you. Express gratitude for the ways He's demonstrated His love toward you.

CHAPTER 6

TURN WORRY ON ITS HEAD

And do not set your heart on what you will eat or drink; do not worry about it.

Luke 12:29

Advertisers have turned our propensity to worry into big business. When they're not appealing to our greed, hunger, or vanity, they're promising freedom from our fears of aging and pain and financial upset and falling behind the fashion trends.

Between global unrest and the local weather, we are barraged by advertisements for products promising to reduce blood sugar, prevent heart attacks, clear skin rashes, restore thinning hair, treat dry mouth, and improve personal hygiene issues. (With, of course, the super speedy, tiny print warning that their products may cause side effects ranging from rash and itching to strokes and suicidal thoughts.)

Between sitcoms and reality TV (an oxymoron if ever there was one), a duck, a gecko, and a few humans guarantee your security and happiness with life insurance, car insurance, medical insurance, homeowners insurance, and short-of-insurance insurance. Nothing left to chance; nothing unknown; nothing to worry about! Except . . . the concerns of Christ's kingdom are completely opposite of the world's. In fact, they're upside down, inside out, and totally backward. Jesus looked to His disciples and said:

Blessed are you who are poor,
     for yours is the kingdom of God.
Blessed are you who hunger now,
     for you will be satisfied.
Blessed are you who weep now,
     for you will laugh.
Blessed are you when people hate you,
     when they exclude you and insult you

> and reject your name as evil, because of the
>   Son of Man.
>
> Rejoice in that day and leap for joy, because
> great is your reward in heaven. For that is how
> their ancestors treated the prophets.
>
> But woe to you who are rich,
>   for you have already received your comfort.
> Woe to you who are well fed now,
>   for you will go hungry.
> Woe to you who laugh now,
>   for you will mourn and weep.
> Woe to you when everyone speaks well of you,
>   for that is how their ancestors treated the
>   false prophets. (Luke 6:20–26)

Christ shakes the earth with these paradigm shifts.

In this Luke passage, which some call the "Sermon on the Plain," Jesus seems to be talking literally. It's better to be poor than rich. It doesn't say "poor in spirit" as the Sermon on the Mount in Matthew records, but just "poor"—as in bills due, checking accounts overdrawn, and layoffs looming. Jesus emphasizes this in His parable about the rich getting to heaven being as impossible as shoving a camel through a needle's eye.

OVERCOMING FEAR AND WORRY

When the disciples heard this, they were greatly astonished and asked, "Who then can be saved?"

Jesus looked at them and said, "With man this is impossible, but with God all things are possible." (Matthew 19:25–26)

Jesus continues with these seismic shifts: It's better to be hungry than well-fed. It's better to cry than to laugh. And it's better to be persecuted than praised.

But He doesn't stop there. The first will be last and the last first (Matthew 19:30); the exalted will be humbled and the humble exalted (Matthew 23:12); and the self-righteous Pharisees and teachers of the law who preside at the temple "will be thrown outside, into the darkness, where there will be weeping and gnashing of teeth" (Matthew 8:12).

The apostle Paul continues this complete reordering of earthly values by claiming:

Whatever were gains to me I now consider loss for the sake of Christ. What is more, I consider everything a loss because of the surpassing worth of knowing Christ Jesus my Lord, for whose sake I have lost all things. I consider them garbage, that I may gain Christ and be found in him. (Philippians 3:7–9)

He emphasizes the worthlessness of his status as a Jew, which at that time was a really big deal. He is essentially discounting his education under the famous rabbi, Gamaliel (see Acts 22:3), and his title of a Pharisee, which were also really big deals.

In fact, he calls it all *scabula*. The Greek word literally means "that which is eliminated," so it could be argued that Paul is saying, compared to knowing Christ, everything else is, well, doodoo.

Earlier in Jesus's teaching recorded in Matthew 6, He warned about the futility of running after food, drink, and clothing. The Father knows we need those things—and has promised them—but also promises something much better. Better than *scabula*.

So much of our worrying is caused by chasing after things that the Bible teaches are unimportant. In fact, Jesus makes it very clear: "What people value highly is detestable in God's sight" (Luke 16:15).

The upside-down kingdom completely changes our priorities. When worry crowds our thinking, we need to replace the world's thinking with productive thinking from God's upside-down kingdom.

Christ over Food and Drink

The Father promises to provide earthly food, but there is something even more valuable in the kingdom:

> I am the living bread that came down from heaven. Whoever eats this bread will live forever. This bread is my flesh, which I will give for the life of the world. (John 6:51)

> Jesus answered, "Everyone who drinks this water will be thirsty again, but whoever drinks the water I give them will never thirst. Indeed, the water I give them will become in them a spring of water welling up to eternal life." (John 4:13–14)

When we worry about food and drink, we may have a mentality of scarcity. We're constantly worried that there won't be enough. Or, in our indulgent culture, we may be worried because we need to cut back on our food intake but it's so hard with temptations all around us. Our mind may be consumed with portion control and food choices and balancing the calorie budget. Either way, whether we are in want or in excess, we need to reorder our thinking in the same way: *He is enough.* Whenever worries about food or drink come to mind, put those worries in perspective by reminding yourself of that spiritual truth. He is enough.

Good Deeds over Clothing

And while the pagans paraded in their fashionable clothing from Ralph Levite and Hebrew Dior, Paul wrote that the truly well-dressed person is wearing something far more valuable:

> I want . . . the women to dress modestly, with decency and propriety, adorning themselves, not with elaborate hairstyles or gold or pearls or expensive clothes, but with good deeds, appropriate for women who profess to worship God. (1 Timothy 2:8–10)

The emphasis here is on not flaunting one's wealth and possessions. Instead of worrying about how we look when we go out, we need to pay attention to what we *do* when we go out. Colossians 3:12 reminds us to "clothe" ourselves with "compassion, kindness, humility, gentleness and patience."

Try this: Next time you choose which shoes to wear outside, also choose what good deed you're going to do while you're out—see if that changes your world more than your footwear. What does this have to do with fear and worry? It's a kind of replacement theory. If your brain is busy with watching for a good deed you can do, it can't be worrying about what you look like. We need to replace worried thoughts with productive thinking from God's upside-down kingdom.

Worship over Savings and Possessions

When I was in elementary school, a local church sign was vandalized. Where once it had proclaimed JESUS SAVES, someone had carefully spray-painted AT FIRST NATIONAL BANK.

It received front-page newspaper coverage and, I'm sure, laughter. But Jesus does offer an incredible savings plan with divine dividends:

> Do not store up for yourselves treasures on earth, where moths and vermin destroy, and where thieves break in and steal. But store up for yourselves treasures in heaven, where moths and vermin do not destroy, and where thieves do not break in and steal. (Matthew 6:19–20)

The more stuff and money we have, the more time it takes to maintain it and protect it—to say nothing of the time it takes to collect it. Here's a quick object lesson: Think about a particular set of shelves in your house. What's on those shelves? Is it easier to keep the shelves clean if they are empty or full? How much time and money went into collecting the items there? How much time and energy do you spend maintaining and protecting what is there? What worries are connected to what's there?—that a child will break something, that a thief will steal it, that a spouse will not put it back where it belongs, that the elements will damage it . . . The fact is, less stuff can amount to less worry, if we let it. With less stuff, our time and energy is less consumed. (That's why I have three pair of shoes: dress shoes, sneakers, and mow-the-lawn sneakers.) We're freer to worship and serve what's worthy of our worship and service.

Eternity over Health

Today we are much more health conscious than we were twenty years ago. And it seems to be working—"forty is the new thirty!" as they say.

Yes, we need to keep the body—the temple of the Holy Spirit—healthy, but Scripture takes a longer-range view of "health."

Therefore we do not lose heart. Though outwardly we are wasting away, yet inwardly we are being renewed day by day. For our light and momentary troubles are achieving for us an eternal glory that far outweighs them all. So we fix our eyes not on what is seen, but on what is unseen, since what is seen is temporary, but what is unseen is eternal. (2 Corinthians 4:16–18)

So will it be with the resurrection of the dead. The body that is sown is perishable, it is raised imperishable; it is sown in dishonor, it is raised in glory; it is sown in weakness, it is raised in power; it is sown a natural body, it is raised a spiritual body. (1 Corinthians 15:42–44)

Health-related fears, both for ourselves and our loved ones, can be among our biggest worries. For some, it's an obsession with staying healthy—devoting resources and time that might be better spent on others to our pursuit of physical fitness. For others, deteriorating health takes its toll and our focus can turn inward, with all of our efforts spent on finding freedom from pain and restriction, which it seems are the world's highest values in those moments. We need to engage in some upside-down thinking, reminding ourselves that these are "light and momentary troubles" when all of our feelings are to the contrary.

Following the world's priorities and values will lead to fear and worry—and worse. Following Jesus's teachings leads to peace!

OVERCOMING STEP
Practice upside-down thinking

You might want to experiment with muting commercials. When a worry comes to mind, consciously consider what Jesus would say to you if He were standing next to you (though He's actually much closer than that). Make sure your priorities are set by Christ's kingdom, not the world's.

CHAPTER 7

DON'T WORRY.
BE HOLY.

But seek first his kingdom and his righteousness.

Matthew 6:33

There's an old preacher's story about a psychologist wanting to determine what makes some children always happy and some perpetually grumpy. The psychologist set up two rooms with the obligatory two-way mirrors and microphones. He filled one with the trendiest toys and the other with a large pile of horse manure.

A five-year-old boy entered the room filled with toys and almost immediately began complaining.

"These toys are dumb! I'm bored. There's nothing to do. Lemme out of here!"

Another five-year-old boy entered the room filled with horse manure and immediately started jumping up and down. "Wow! I'm the luckiest kid in the world! I can't believe this. This is great!" The shocked researcher dropped his clipboard and opened the microphone into the room. "Young man, what are you so happy about?"

"With all this horse manure, there's got to be pony!"

I'm sure it's an apocryphal anecdote, but it does make the point: much of our reaction to life is perspective. You probably know people who are thrilled to find a quarter in the Walmart parking lot. Then there are those who could win a half-billion lottery prize and complain that they're going to have to pay taxes.

The Right Mind-Set

The key to a worry-free life is not our surroundings but in what our mind is set on: "You will keep in perfect peace all who trust in you, all whose thoughts are fixed on you!" (Isaiah 26:3 NLT).

The Hebrew word translated as "fixed" is *sâmak*, which means to lean upon, lay on, or rest upon. The King James Version reads "stayed on." When our minds stay on God, we will experience "perfect peace." That Hebrew word is *shâlôm*, and it conveys completeness, soundness, welfare, peace which leads to safety, prosperity, tranquility, and contentment. Perfect indeed!

David's response to a taunting Goliath provides a great illustration for this kind of mind-set. David certainly had plenty to worry about in facing off with a guy many times bigger, fiercer, and better equipped. "Come here," Goliath said, "and I'll give your flesh to the birds and the wild animals!" (1 Samuel 17:43–44).

But David's mind was fixed:

> You come against me with sword and spear and javelin, but I come against you in the name of the LORD Almighty, the God of the armies of Israel, whom you have defied. This day the LORD will deliver you into my hands, and I'll strike you down and cut off your head. This very day I will give the carcasses of the Philistine army to the birds and the wild animals, and the whole world will know that there is a God in Israel. All those gathered here will know that it is not by sword or spear that the LORD saves; for the battle is the LORD's, and he will give all of you into our hands. (1 Samuel 17:45–47)

As you know, it was Goliath who became a buzzard buffet. We too have a choice whose promises and power we will believe—our enemy's or our God's:

"You're out of work and you deserve to suffer" or
"I will meet all your needs."

"Your prodigal children have wandered too far to be saved" or
"I want all people to be saved."

"You can't do it" or
"I am your refuge and strength, and am always present to help."

"You're all alone" or
"I am with you wherever you go."

"You'll always be a worrier" or
"I give you my peace."

The Rule of Peace

The apostle Paul wrote a lot about how we experience God's peace in our hearts and minds. In his letter to the church at Colossae, we read: "Let the peace of Christ rule in your hearts, since as members of one body you were called to peace. And be thankful" (Colossians 3:15).

The Greek word for "rule" is *brabeúō*, meaning to umpire, decide, determine, direct, control, or rule. I like the idea of Christ being the umpire of our thoughts. He's calling out what thoughts are foul, out of bounds, or need to be ejected from our minds. As we allow the peace of Christ to rule in our hearts, "the peace of God, which transcends all understanding, will guard" our hearts and minds (Philippians 4:7).

Paul provides a helpful list in Philippians 4:8 of those things we should allow to occupy our minds so we can experience God's peace of mind:

- whatever is true
- whatever is noble
- whatever is right
- whatever is pure
- whatever is lovely
- whatever is admirable
- anything excellent
- anything praiseworthy

When our children were small we posted that list on our TV. It was a great teaching tool when something came on that didn't line up with the list. So, years later, while watching a popular sitcom with excellent writing, humor, and acting, I started going down the list.

Right? Nope. It overtly promoted atheism, moral relativism, and evolution.

Pure? Nope. The characters were hopping in and out of bed like rabbits.

Lovely? We may be confused by this word that brings to mind decorator towels, an elaborately set table, or DIY Pinterest projects. In the Greek the word means "motivated to love." Did the actions of the characters demonstrate love? Would they motivate me to love? Some were actually loving, caring people who treated the other characters with respect and dignity. However, other characters treated others as sexual objects and had the morals of a tomcat.

Admirable? Would I want my children and grandchildren to model their lives after the characters? No way!

Excellent? Unlike so many "Christian" television shows and films, this show had believable dialogue, excellent acting, and great production value, so I gave it a thumbs-up for excellence.

Praiseworthy? Although I thoroughly enjoyed the show—and many of my believing friends were huge fans—I had to admit that while it did have some good qualities, overall it failed the should-I-set-my-mind-on-this test.

Worry occurs when we fail to fix our minds on the godly values in Paul's list. Fears take over when we dwell on the enemy's lies rather than God's promises.

True and noble? Our world is filled with rumors, fake news, conspiracy theories, and the latest gossip.

Right, pure, and lovely? Most television programming and films are not based on what Christians should think about. Right-wing and left-wing talk shows and internet forums do not "motivate toward love." On the contrary, an interesting discovery came out of the Chapman University study that we looked at in chapter 1: "Watching television talk shows with frequency proved to be strongly related to fear."

Yes, some talk show topics are, shall we say, *interesting*: The United States is secretly run by a mysterious "deep state"; many elected officials are shapeshifting lizards; and what appear to be jet trails are actually government-spread toxins designed to turn Americans into brainwashed zombies. (No wonder zombies made Chapman's list.)

However, even on the less *interesting* talk shows there's enough to feed the fears documented by the Chapman study: climate change, gun violence, government corruption, the ever-increasing national debt . . .

Why do we watch them? Is it enough if they simply pass the "true" test? Do they motivate us to love or to worry?

According to Dr. Bader, a sociology professor at Chapman, "It is a simple, straight-line effect—the more one watches talk TV, the more fearful one tends to be." He points out that it's not clear whether TV makes people more fearful or whether more fearful people watch more TV. Either way, it's worth some Spirit-driven self-examination.

Our list could go on. How many leaders in our world are truly *admirable*? How much of our art and music—even "Christian" art and music—is *excellent* and *praiseworthy*?

Paul would warn, do not set your mind on these lesser things.

As mentioned earlier, God gives power to overcome worry and fear. One powerful verse, Philippians 4:13, has been wrenched from its context and made to teach we "can do all things" through Christ, from raising money for church building projects to losing weight. That's not what it's about.

I am not saying this because I am in need, for I have learned to be content whatever the circumstances. I know what it is to be in need, and I know what it is to have plenty. I have learned the secret of being content in any and every situation, whether well fed or hungry, whether living in plenty or in want. I can do all this through him who gives me strength. (Philippians 4:11–13)

Christ gave Paul the "strength" to be content—to not worry—in good and bad circumstances. That's the context of the verse. And it's a strength that He will give us also.

OVERCOMING STEP
Cultivate peace of mind

What situations feed your worry habit? Are any of those situations avoidable—like listening to talk radio? Write out Philippians 4:6–7 and Philippians 4:8 on two index cards each, and place them in strategic spots where you need the visual reminder.

CHAPTER 8

MIND OVER WORRY

If that is how God clothes the grass of the field, which is here today and tomorrow is thrown into the fire, will he not much more clothe you—you of little faith?

Matthew 6:30

In the film *City Slickers*, Curly (Jack Palance), the trail boss, asks Mitch (Billy Crystal), the city slicker, "Do you know what the secret of life is? This." Curly points up with his index finger.

"Your finger?"
"One thing. Just one thing."
"But, what is the 'one thing?'"
"That's what you have to figure out."

The story of Mary and Martha emphasizes what that One Thing is. Martha was famous throughout Bethany for her home-decorating and party-planning—truly a first-century Martha Stewart. Now, the most respected teacher in all Palestine was coming for dinner, along with His twelve disciples.

> She had a sister called Mary, who sat at the Lord's feet listening to what he said. But Martha was distracted by all the preparations that had to be made. She came to him and asked, "Lord, don't you care that my sister has left me to do the work by myself? Tell her to help me!"
>
> "Martha, Martha," the Lord answered, "you are worried and upset about many things, but few things are needed—or indeed only one. Mary has chosen what is better, and it will not be taken away from her." (Luke 10:39–42)

As we started to unpack in the prior chapter, much of our worrying derives from concentrating on the wrong things. Rather than enjoying the presence of Jesus, Martha was scurrying around the kitchen, worried and upset, trying to make an elaborate feast when He simply wanted one thing: to spend time with the sisters and their brother, Lazarus.

"The mind governed by the flesh is death," writes Paul, "but the mind governed by the Spirit is life and peace" (Romans 8:6). We may be thinking about good things, but how do we know if our mind is governed by the Spirit? Here are some questions to consider:

- When you wake up in the morning, what is your mind programmed to rehearse?
- When life is moving along smoothly, what is the default setting of your thoughts?
- When you have pressures on your life, what is your mind's auto response?
- When you're performing mindless tasks, where does your mind's autopilot take you?

There are several theories of how we change ingrained behavior. And worry is fundamentally a bad habit. The first is known as cognitive theory. It involves a cognitive, affective, and behavioral component, but for me, it's so much easier to call the steps . . .

Know → Feel → Do

I learn something new. I feel it's something good for me and I desire to do it. Then, I do it.

Cognitive dissonance theory is similar.

Know → Feel Bad → Do

This is simply good, old-fashioned *conviction*. God reveals an area that needs work; I feel bad about it, and I'm faced with a choice—change or refuse to change. The theory argues that we humans cannot live with dissonance—or conflict—between our beliefs and our behaviors, and so we strive for "balance." We see this in the very first converts on the day of Pentecost:

> Then Peter stood up with the Eleven, raised his voice and addressed the crowd: "Fellow Jews and all of you who live in Jerusalem, let me explain this to you; listen carefully to what I say." (Acts 2:14)

First, Peter told them something, so that they would *know* what was true.

> When the people heard this, they were cut to the heart [*feel*] and said to Peter and the other apostles, "Brothers, what shall we do?" [*do*]. (2:37)

The crowd was faced with a choice, and about three thousand people made the right choice that day (2:38–41).

We too are faced with a choice. We know that worry is sin. We feel badly about worrying. Now we need to choose either to continue in our sin or to stop. While the ideal would be to do what is right, unfortunately, we can attempt resolution by denying or distorting the conviction.

"God really didn't mean that I should stop worrying" or "I don't worry, I'm simply—as the government tells us all to be—vigilant."

And sometimes—as Paul wrote—we know what we feel, but we just don't act on it:

> I have the desire to do what is good [*stop worrying*], but I cannot carry it out. For I do not do the good I want to do, but the evil [*worry*] I do not want to do—this I keep on doing. (Romans 7:18–19)

Then the dissonance continues, and there's no peace in that. Sometimes our feelings just don't come in line with what we know is right. *I know I should stop [insert any sinful behavior], but I just don't want to.* I don't want to act loving. I don't want to forgive. I don't want to stop worrying. For those situations, we need this formula:

Know → Do → Feel

Or to put it more simply, "Fake it till you make it!"

I tried this one week. Instead of worrying about my income as a freelance writer, I determined to simply praise God for His provisions and not ask for one single thing. I picked the wrong week!

Monday, I discovered we had a little over one hundred dollars in our account and bills amounting to over a thousand dollars. Wednesday a publisher that owed me several hundred dollars in back royalties announced that it too was broke.

Doubt

I wish there was a more flattering word for what I was feeling! While I *knew* the truth of Scripture, I just didn't trust that it would work in this instance. I *doubted* that God had a plan and that He was already working for the good (Romans 8:28) to provide for us. It was up to *me* to keep myself, my wife, and two kids from living in a cardboard box! So I frantically brainstormed ways to cut expenses and generate more income: sell my books on the street corner, pawn my guitars, and give up dark chocolate.

Oswald Chambers asks, "Can you trust Jesus Christ where your common sense cannot trust Him? Can you venture out with courage on the words of Jesus Christ, while the realities of your commonsense life continue to shout, 'It's all a lie'?"[1]

Determination

By midweek—after serious Bible reading, prayer, and writing out my angst in my journal—I finally got a grip. (The thought of giving up dark chocolate brought me to my senses.)

God had been faithful and had always provided unexpected income, whether from jobs and projects that appeared seemingly from nowhere to surprising inheritances from family friends. I willfully, deliberately determined to trust that God would do the same this time as well. White-knuckled trust is better than yellow-streaked doubt, right?

But King David described a higher level of faith than simply trust:

> Trust in the LORD and do good.
>   Then you will live safely in the land and
>   prosper.
> Take delight in the LORD,
>   and he will give you your heart's desires.
>   (Psalm 37:3–4 NLT)

David invites us to trust, act on that trust, and, the icing on the cake, delight in God.

Delight

By Thursday, I was still determined to trust and praise God and was actually feeling a twinge of delight that God had this covered. I had been meditating on Ephesians 3:20's promise that God is able to do immeasurably more than all we ask or imagine. (As a writer, I have a pretty good imagination.)

God certainly doesn't want us to doubt His power to provide, but He wants us to go beyond simply determined trust to joyful delight in His care. So I began making a list of all the surprising ways God in the past had pulled a rabbit out of the hat when everything looked black and empty. I actually broke into my happy dance.

Friday I was still trying to delight in God—while on my way to the bank to hock our car for a loan to cover our bills. On the way, I stopped by my daughter's school to pay her tuition. But it turned out there had been an error last semester, and we didn't owe money that month. Praise the Lord!

My next stop was at a Christian university to check on some advertising copy I had recently written. "That was great," the director announced.

"We'd also like you to rewrite all our admissions brochures. Do you think you could do that for around a thousand dollars?" Praise the Lord!

I never did get to the bank. All our bills were paid!

I wish I could say I am constantly, consistently at the stage of delight. But my head and heart still sometimes conflict, just like when I watched *The Lone Ranger* as a child.

Right now I *know* that I'm going to make the deadline for this book. But in my heart is a small, nagging worry that says "You won't make the deadline. You'll never get another book contract. You'll spend the rest of your life writing really depressing poetry at a homeless shelter."

Fear is an emotional black hole that not only swallows up peace, joy, and delight but also sucks up energy and creativity. So I'm trying to expend my energy on trust rather than fear. And—you may want to underline this—trust and worry require the same amount of mental, emotional, and spiritual energy.

Do is willfully and deliberately choosing to act with trust over fear.

I tell myself that Jesus has commanded me not to worry about it, and if He has commanded it, He has equipped me to obey. By His death and resurrection and the infilling of the Spirit, I have all the resources I need to do God's work.

Despite what my thoughts, hormones, or the cold pizza I had for breakfast is telling me, I can *do* the next right thing. I can *decide* to act in faith. Remember, it's not the amount of faith you have, but that you act on it.

OVERCOMING STEP
Decide to act in faith

Make a list of things you sense God asking you to do—no matter how much they defy common sense. Then pick one and do it.

CHAPTER 9

POWER OVER WORRY

Do not worry about tomorrow, for tomorrow will worry about itself. Each day has enough trouble of its own.

Matthew 6:34

When my son and daughter were small, they loved Advent calendars. Not only was it a visual way to keep track of how many days until the Christmas-gift-giving extravaganza, but behind each door was a small treat. My wife and I were constantly reminding them to keep tomorrow's door closed.

Today, my daughter is a licensed therapist who teaches her clients to keep the door of tomorrow locked and focus on today. Focusing on the current moment is beneficial for pain management, addictions, depression, and the general worry of life. It rejects multitasking; it's living out the moment in the moment. It's a conscious acceptance that today is the only day we have any influence over. Focusing on yesterday often brings regrets. And looking forward to tomorrow actually has two dangers:

1. It causes worry about future events (which may or may not even happen).
2. It causes us to not savor the life we have.

Jesus is clear: "Do not worry about tomorrow for tomorrow will worry about itself. Each day has enough trouble of its own." When it comes to worry, we need to keep tomorrow's door closed.

Jesus's brother, James, also cautions us against dwelling on the future:

Now listen, you who say, "Today or tomorrow we will go to this or that city, spend a year there, carry on business and make money." Why, you do not even know what will happen tomorrow. What is your life? You are a mist that appears for a little while and then vanishes. Instead, you ought to say, "If it is the

Lord's will, we will live and do this or that." As it is, you boast in your arrogant schemes. All such boasting is evil. (James 4:13–16)

It today's vernacular, obsessing and worrying about tomorrow instead of enjoying the gift of today is "future tripping." Yep, we're all guilty of tripping over the future.

When I'm tempted to worry about tomorrow and beyond, I mentally talk myself off the ledge by appreciating the gifts of today:

Today, I'm warm and well-fed. I'm living in a country with resources to keep me from starving. I have a reliable vehicle—even if it has 212,000 miles on it. (Its name is Bob, short for Bucket Of Bolts.) I have a closet full of clothes. I have a roof over my head—actually a three-bedroom home in the suburbs. And I am free to write Christian books without the government sending me to a forced labor camp. Today—at this moment— everything is great!

I could say a lot more, but you get the idea. Like advertisements, I do need to provide some disclaimers: (1) This doesn't mean I don't pay the mortgage due next week or renew my internet and cell phone service for another month. I dutifully prepare for my earthly responsibilities and obligations. (2) There's value in rehearsing the past in order to focus on God's faithfulness. (3) While we're not to invite *worry* about tomorrow, we are encouraged by the *hope* we have for our eternal future—it's okay to dwell on that!

What it does mean is that, wherever I am, I am there. If I'm playing a board game with my grand-kiddos, I am not thinking about how I really need to be working on that worry book. When I'm out on a date with my wife, I'm not checking my text messages. (Lois and I actually sat in the booth across from a young couple in a nice restaurant. For the entire meal, they were individually staring at their phones.) It means I'm not writing a grocery list in the Sermon Notes section of the church bulletin.

I *was* one of the worst, so I'm not trying to send you on a guilt trip. I would watch the evening news, computer in my lap, checking email as I ate my dinner. There were times when I finished my meal without even being conscious of the taste or smell of the mega-meat pizza! I find I'm enjoying food much more when I'm focused on the taste, texture, and smell of the crispy crust, the sweet tomato sauce, the tingle of pepperoni, the . . . well, you get the point. I can actually remember the news items I just watched because I'm not checking Facebook during the news. I'm not perfect. I still tend to play electronic games while watching TV, but I am intentionally trying to live for today and all the treasures it offers.

God is the only being who can exist in the past, present, and future. The psalmist writes, "All the days ordained for me were written in your book before one of them came to be" (Psalm 139:16). Because *He* holds the future, I can hold today without worry. I can fully experience and enjoy every person, conversation, situation, and mega-meat pizza. I can enjoy *now*, because God holds the past and future.

Corrie ten Boom, a concentration camp survivor, puts it well: "Worry does not empty tomorrow of its sorrow, it empties today of its strength." So keep the door to tomorrow locked. But, like everything else, we can't do this in our own strength; we need the Holy Spirit's power. These disciplines will help you to *know* God and *do* His will and *feel* His peace.

Scripture Reading

Regularly reading the Bible is absolutely essential in keeping our minds fixed on God. You can't read the Word and worry at the same time!

Psalm 119:165 declares: "Great peace have those who love your law, and nothing can make them stumble."

Paul writes: "For everything that was written in the past was written to teach us, so that through the endurance taught in the Scriptures and the encouragement they provide we might have hope" (Romans 15:4).

May I suggest you schedule an inviolable time to read God's Word? You will never "find time" for the Bible, so you have to make it. It doesn't have to be long, but it needs to be consistent. And you need a plan. With the various Bible apps, you can read God's Word anywhere, any way; through the Bible in a year, chronologically, by topics—there are lots of options.

Whatever plan you choose, I would recommend you approach the Bible like Google Maps, although God's Word is infinitely more accurate. Get the satellite view from thirty thousand feet to understand an individual book's theme. After that, press the + icon to narrow in on individual chapters. Then, finally, zoom in on the individual words and their meanings.

As you read, look for the takeaway God wants you to . . . well, *take away* and apply to your life. I am amazed at how many times the next passage in my reading plan is exactly applicable to the challenge I'm facing right then. It's as though the plan was custom-designed for my life. How does God do that?!

BibleGateway.com is my go-to Bible. There, you'll find various translations as well as study helps. BibleHub.com has a good selection of commentaries for discovering word meanings and the cultural context of a passage. And StudyLight.org is an excellent way to learn the nuanced meanings of the Hebrew, Aramaic, and Greek words.

Prayer

I'm learning that listening is the most important element of prayer.

> "My soul waits in silence for God only." (Psalm 62:1 NASB)

> "It is good to wait quietly for the salvation of the LORD. . . . Let him sit alone in silence." (Lamentations 3:26, 28)

> "Be still, and know that I am God." (Psalm 46:10)

After I finished my previous book, all I heard when I tried to pray was "be still." Now, for a Type A workaholic with ADD who writes and speaks for a living, that is not easy. But I saw it everywhere—in reading Scripture, on Facebook and Instagram posts, on wall plaques and bookmarks, and in music such as Hillary Scott's powerful song "Still." A writer friend sent me her latest book with "Be Still" in the subtitle!

After five months of trying to be still, I thought, *Maybe God wants me to write on being still.* I was sure I could hear God chuckling, "Jim, Jim, Jim."

So for nine long months I simply read the Bible and classic devotional books, prayed, journaled, and *tried* to be still. I learned so much. And then Discovery House asked me to write this book. I was refreshed and worry-free and ready to tackle the assignment.

Rather than bringing your five-page prayer list to God, try simply being still and allow God to speak to you. Let Him give you the assurance, peace, and comfort that He's working on those concerns and even now is working all out for your good and His glory (Romans 8:28–29).

Journaling

I've described my journal as the sock drawer of my mind. I write insights from my daily Bible and devotional readings, encouraging quotations from social media and Dove chocolate wrappers, funny things my grandchildren say, prayer requests and answers.

I highly recommend journaling because (1) it's a record of your spiritual growth and all the amazing ways God has met your needs over the years, (2) it's a family history with great stories that will be told long after you're gone, (3) it contains notes of encouragement from others for when you're feeling completely useless, and most of all, (4) it's a really cheap form of therapy. Really!

Studies have noted that fifteen to twenty minutes of expressive writing on a handful of occasions was enough to help study participants deal with traumatic, stressful, or otherwise emotional events.[1] Like diet and exercise, it's been linked to improved mood and memory. There's even a Center for Journal Therapy online, dedicated to the mental health benefits of regular journaling, both in therapeutic and personal settings.

For me, the best part of journaling is reading of all the ways God has provided for me through two layoffs from the perfect jobs in publishing, cancer, four surgeries in three hospitals in two months, parental purgatory, and dealing with my mental health issues of clinical depression, a touch of autism, ADD, and

OCD. I'm still standing! So when I'm tempted to worry, I can go to my journal and discover I've been through worse, and—by the grace of God—came out victorious.

Meditation

Given how our minds resemble pinball machines with schedules, appointments, to-do lists, deadlines, and meetings ricocheting inside our skulls, it's no wonder the Bible urges us to meditate. This is not Eastern meditation where we assume the lotus position and attempt to empty our minds. No way, "namaste." Instead, we fill our minds and lips with thoughts of God's law and His attributes, especially His unfailing love.

> Test me, LORD, and try me,
> examine my heart and my mind;
> for I have always been mindful of your unfail-
> ing love
> and have lived in reliance on your faithfulness.
> (Psalm 26:2–3)

> Keep this Book of the Law always on your lips; meditate on it day and night, so that you may be careful to do everything written in it.

Then you will be prosperous and successful. (Joshua 1:8)

Within your temple, O God,
we meditate on your unfailing love. (Psalm 48:9)

I have more insight than all my teachers,
for I meditate on your statutes. (Psalm 119:99)

One Hebrew word for "meditate" is *sîyach*, which means to put forth, muse, commune, speak, complain, study, ponder, or sing. It's used in Psalm 119:15—"I will meditate on your precepts and consider your ways." Another word is *hâgâh*, which means to moan, growl, utter, muse, mutter, meditate, devise, plot, or speak. It's used in Joshua 1:8—"Keep this Book of the Law always on your lips; meditate on it day and night." Meditation does not need to be silent! Psalm 77:12 uses both words:

I will consider [*sîyach*] all your works
and meditate [*hâgâh*] on all your mighty deeds.

So meditate on God and His Word and His mighty deeds. Muse over them, study and ponder them, speak of them, mutter them, sing them. Speaking of singing . . .

Music

God is a great DJ. When I put on my headphones and crank up the contemporary Christian music channel on Pandora, it seems the songs are perfectly planned for what I struggle with at that moment. I know, I know, it's a computer algorithm based on my likes and dislikes selecting the music. But my theology also allows for God to somehow orchestrate the playlist while I'm listening.

Like David's soothing harp music calmed the mentally deranged King Saul, so music calms our mental turmoil. It relaxes and encourages us.

I've included some of my favorite anti-worry songs at this book's website: www.jameswatkins .com/OvercomingFearAndWorry.

Gathering Together

My favorite time in one of our churches was testimony time. Parishioners had the opportunity to share what God had done in their life during the past week. No one could say, "I was saved and sanctified twenty years ago." It had to be something current. I loved hearing of answers to prayers for changed lives, new jobs, and prodigal children coming home.

One of the best ways to deal with worry is to be with fellow strugglers who have been through what currently worries you and have seen God work in amazing ways, to enjoy the fellowship of their prayers, and to feel the power of God's work done in community.

So be involved in a local church's Sunday school class or small group. A group that will accept you, worry warts and all, is a great prescription to combat worry.

OVERCOMING STEP
Practice spiritual disciplines

1. For six days, block out a specific time each day to be alone with God, your Bible, and a journal. (Then do it.)
2. On the seventh day, journal about any changes you've seen in your worry habit as you've attempted to be present in the moment. Write out a faith-based prayer, letting God know . . . that you know . . . that He's got everything under control. Thank Him profusely.
3. Repeat steps 1 and 2 indefinitely.

YOU ARE NOT ALONE

You will receive power when the Holy Spirit comes on you. . . .

Acts 1:8

The disciples had been through a stressful three years. The Holmes-Rahe Stress Inventory lists different events in our lives and assigns a number to rank the impact of each event: everything from death of spouse (100) to major holidays (12). When a person reaches 200 points within a year, he or she is in danger of physically breaking down.

In the first year the disciples were with Jesus, they racked up a whole spreadsheet of stress numbers:

- Major change in financial state (from regular employment to handouts): 38
- Changing to different line of work (a line of work that previously didn't exist): 36
- Major change in responsibilities at work: 29
- Outstanding personal achievement (healing and casting out demons): 28
- Major change in living conditions (no security or predictability): 25
- Revision of personal habits (separated from family): 24
- Major change in working hours or conditions (being on call 24/7): 20
- Change in residence (on the road): 20
- Major change in church activity: 19
- Major holidays (seven Jewish festivals every year; 12 points for each): 84

That's 323 points worth of stress in just the first year! And then over the next couple years there was the shift in their understanding of God's law, crowds begging for healing, the anger and rejection of disbelievers, and the fear of near-drowning. Until finally, they faced Jesus's death, burial, and resurrection, and the resulting chaos, all of which would have been heart-pounding, life-changing, emotional experiences.

And then Jesus reappeared and announced He was leaving them with the responsibility to "go and make disciples of all nations, baptizing them in the name of the Father and of the Son and of the Holy Spirit, and teaching them to obey everything I have commanded you" (Matthew 28:19–20).

They must have felt worried about being abandoned with a responsibility way beyond their ability to accomplish. And, since you picked up this book, you too have issues causing worry and stress. (You can tally your own stress score at www.stress.org.)

But here's the good news I want you to remember as we finish up here. As Jesus left the disciples with a big task, He left them with a promise. And His promise for them is also a promise for us:

"Surely I am with you always, to the very end of the age." (Matthew 28:20)

"You will receive power when the Holy Spirit comes on you." (Acts 1:8)

While worry is something Jesus commands us to not do, He doesn't leave us helpless. He will actually come and live within you "always" and, through His Spirit, "you will receive power" to trust Him completely. And everyone said "Amen."

APPENDIX

WORRY OR ANXIETY?

I was sick and you looked after me.

Matthew 25:36

When someone tells me that I should just think more positively about my clinical depression, mild autism, and OCD, I am tempted to tell them to just think more positively about their glaucoma, high blood pressure, or diabetes. But of course I don't.

Instead, I try to explain how the fall (Genesis 3) has even affected our minds with biochemical deformities causing Alzheimer's disease and other dementia, bi-polar disorders, clinical depression, and—yes—even anxiety.

Many people, even healthcare professionals, use the word *anxiety* loosely as a synonym for *worry*. But diagnosable anxiety—what they may call *anxiety disorder*—is more than just worry. The difference is in anxiety's intensity and biochemical element.

Pastor Stephen Altrogge writes in a blog post about his struggles with chronic physical anxiety: "I regularly experience a clutching sensation in my chest, shortness of breath, adrenaline surges, and a sick feeling in the pit of my stomach." Sometimes there's something he's actually worried about, but 90 percent of the time there's not. The sensations just come out of nowhere.

> In those moments, I don't need to be told not to worry. I don't need to be told to exercise more faith in the promises of God. I don't need to be told to snap out of it. What I need is encouragement to persevere. I need to be reminded that, even in the midst of suffering, Jesus is near. I need to be reminded that my light and momentary afflictions are producing an eternal weight of glory. I need to be encouraged to press into Jesus.
>
> And . . . I need to be connected to someone who can help me deal with the physical aspects of anxiety.

The physical aspects of anxiety are not likely to just go away on their own, any more than chronic pain sufferers can expect their pain to disappear on its own. So, how can we tell if we're dealing with worry or full-blown anxiety? Here are some of the broad differences:

1. Worry is a mental activity; anxiety has a physical cause and effect.
2. Worry is specific; anxiety is generalized and vague.

There are specific issues with worry, such as getting to the airport and through security in time. Anxiety can be a generalized fear that we can't put our finger on, but we feel anxious as we board the plane.

When anxiety escalates, it can defy logic. A realistic worry may be that we will be seated next to a talkative passenger when we don't like to talk to strangers and just want to read our novel. An anxiety disorder may have us filled with terror that we will be seated next to a suicide bomber.

3. Worry often leads us to brainstorm a solution to its source; anxiety can lead to panic, helplessness, and despair.

4. Worry creates mild emotional distress; anxiety causes severe, debilitating emotional distress.

Anxiety can cause us to avoid social situations, be afraid to leave the house, or even be unable to continue in our job. If it's affecting your relationships and career, you should seek help from a healthcare professional.

5. Although a tendency to worry can be a long-term struggle, worry over each specific issue will likely be temporary—until the issue is resolved; anxiety is more prolonged.

As with clinical depression, if feelings of fear and anxiety continue for more than two weeks—especially without an identifiable, specific, or realistic trigger—see your health care professional. It may be a true mental health issue requiring psychological treatment or medication.

Similarly, make a doctor's appointment if you have any of these symptoms:

- Trouble sleeping. You collapse into bed dead tired, but then find yourself wide awake with worry.

- Waking up tired and tiredness throughout the day. Even when you do have a full night's sleep, all the coffee in Colombia can't seem to give you enough energy.

- Experiencing food cravings. Adrenaline overdrive causes your body to crave sweet and salty foods to provide energy and replenish our systems. While I was having radiation treatments for cancer, I developed an insatiable appetite for dill pickles. I don't particularly like them, but I was devouring them like a pregnant woman! As soon as the stress of radiation treatments was over, the cravings were gone.

- Gaining belly fat. That "spare tire" may be a sign that your body is producing too much stress hormone—cortisol.

- Becoming the grizzly bear. There may actually be a physical reason for our feeling tense, highly judgmental, and suspicious—what a friend calls "witchy." As mentioned earlier, in fight-or-flight mode, we develop laser-focused vision and our hearing is diminished. We see only what's wrong with everyone within range. We become the grizzly bear!

I can assure you there is help. Thanks to prayer and Prozac, I can actually get out of bed rather than hiding under the covers eating my body weight of dark chocolate. It's still not easy. When I awake in the morning to my mental tornado, I think "worry" as I breathe out, and "Jesus" as I breathe in. It takes several minutes of intense concentration for the twister to stop spinning and a calm, quiet peace to come to mind. But it can be done! I just wish I had been diagnosed twenty years earlier.

NOTES

Chapter 1

1. Michael J. Peterson, "Generalized Anxiety Disorder (GAD)," MedicineNet, accessed December 19, 2018, www.medicinenet.com /anxiety/article.htm#what_is_anxiety.

2. James Watkins, *Squeezing Good Out of Bad* (Raleigh, NC: Lighthouse Publishing of the Carolinas, 2014), 15–20.

3. "America's Top Fears 2018: Chapman University Survey of American Fears," Wilkinson College of Arts, Humanities, and Social Sciences blog, Earl Babbie Research Center, October 16, 2018, https:// blogs.chapman.edu/wilkinson/2018/10/16/americas-top-fears-2018/. The full report can be seen at https://www.chapman.edu/wilkinson /research-centers/babbie-center/_files/fear-2018/fear-V-methodology -report-ssrs.pdf.

4. Sheri Ledbetter, "What Americans Fear Most—New Poll from Chapman University," Chapman University Press Room, October 20, 2014, https://blogs.chapman.edu/press-room/2014/10/20 /what-americans-fear-most-new-poll-from-chapman-university/.

5. Robyn Rapoport and Kyle Berta, "Methodology Report: American Fears Survey July 2018," https://www.chapman.edu/wilkinson/research -centers/babbie-center/_files/fear-2018/fear-V-methodology-report-ssrs .pdf, pp. 97, 35, respectively.

Chapter 2

1. See Matthew 5:21–22, 28, 43–48.

2. See Matthew 14:22–31; Matthew 16:21–23; Matthew 26:31–35, 69–75.

3. Colossians 1:15–27.

4. A(lbert) B(enjamin) Simpson, *Days of Heaven on Earth: A Daily Devotional to Comfort and Inspire* (Chicago: Moody Bible Institute, 1984), August 23 entry.

5. See Psalm 56:2–3; Daniel 10:7–8; Matthew 8:26; 14:30; 28:8; Acts 18:9; 2 Corinthians 12:20.

Chapter 3

1. See Nicole M. Talge, Charles Neal, and Vivette Glover, "Antenatal Maternal Stress and Long-Term Effect on Child Neurodevelopment: How and Why? *J Child Psychol Psychiatry* (Mar–Apr 2007) 48(3-4): 245–61, DOI: 10.1111/j.1469-7610.2006.01714.x.

2. Seth J. Gillihan, "5 Reasons We Worry, and 5 Ways to Worry Less," Psychology Today blog, October 7, 2016, psychologytoday.com/us /blog/think-act-be/201610/5-reasons-we-worry-and-5-ways-worry-less.

3. Gillihan, "5 Reasons."

4. Gillihan, "5 Reasons."

5. Gillihan, "5 Reasons."

6. Psalm 43:5

Chapter 4

1. Eric J. Olson, "Lack of Sleep: Can It Make You Sick?" Mayo Clinic FAQ, accessed November 19, 2018, https://www.mayoclinic.org /diseases-conditions/insomnia/expert-answers/lack-of-sleep/faq-20057757.

2. National Sleep Foundation, "The Complex Relation-ship Between Sleep, Depression & Anxiety," accessed December 19, 2018, www.sleepfoundation.org/excessivesleepiness/content /the-complex-relationship-between-sleep-depression-anxiety.

Chapter 5

1. *The New Testament in Modern English* by J.B. Phillips copyright © 1960, 1972 J. B. Phillips. Administered by The Archbishops' Council of the Church of England. Used by permission.

ABOUT THE AUTHOR

James Watkins is the author of over 20 books and 2,000 articles as well as a conference speaker who has traveled around the world sharing "hope and humor." Four of his books have received national industry awards, as well as five awards from the Evangelical Press Association. He has served as an editor at three publishers and taught writing at Taylor University for fifteen years. Most of all he loves God, his family, writing and speaking, and Chinese food—in that order. Learn more about Jim at hopeandhumor.org. For additional resources for overcoming worry, visit www.jameswatkins.com/OvercomingFearAndWorry.

Other books by James Watkins

The Psalms of Aspah: Struggling with Unanswered Prayer, Unfulfilled Promises, and Unpunished Evil
The Imitation of Christ: Classic Devotions in Today's Language
Squeezing Good Out of Bad

Help us get the word out!

Our Daily Bread Publishing exists to feed the soul
with the Word of God.

If you appreciated this book, please let others know.

- Pick up another copy to give as a gift.

- Share a link to the book or mention it
  on social media.

- Write a review on your blog, on a book-
  seller's website, or at our own site
  (odb.org/store).

- Recommend this book for your church,
  book club, or small group.

Connect with us:

 @ourdailybread

 @ourdailybread

🐦 @ourdailybread

Our Daily Bread Publishing
PO Box 3566
Grand Rapids, Michigan 49501 USA

✉ books@odb.org

2. *The Living Bible* copyright © 1971 by Tyndale House Foundation. Used by permission of Tyndale House Publishers Inc., Carol Stream, Illinois 60188. All right reserved.

Chapter 8

1. Oswald Chambers, "The Unsurpassed Intimacy of Tested Faith," in *My Utmost for His Highest*, updated edition, ed. James Reimann (Grand Rapids: Discovery House, 1992), August 29 entry.

Chapter 9

1. Karen A. Baikie and Kay Wilhelm, "Emotional and Physical Health Benefits of Expressive Writing," *Advances in Psychiatric Treatment* 11, no. 5 (September 2005), https://doi.org/10.1192/apt.11.5.338.